# NNAT®
# GRADE 3
## NNAT3 Level D

**ABOUT ORIGINS PUBLICATIONS**

Origins Publications helps students develop their higher-order thinking skills while also improving their chances of admission into gifted and accelerated learner programs.

Our goal is to unleash and nurture the genius in every student. We do this by offering educational and test prep materials that are fun, challenging and provide a sense of accomplishment.

Please contact us with any questions.
info@originspublications.com

Copyright© 2019 by Origins Publications
Written and Edited by: Gifted and Talented NNAT Test Prep Team

ISBN: 978-1-948255-84-4

# BONUS

## DOWNLOAD YOUR NNAT PRACTICE TEST

## IN

# COLOR

If you also want the COLOR version of this book, please go to the following link to download it!

Please visit
**https://originstutoring.lpages.co/nnat150**

to access the color version of the practice test.

# Contents

# Part 1: Introduction to the NNAT®

This book offers an overview of the types of questions on the Naglieri Nonverbal Ability Test (NNAT) Level D, test-taking strategies to improve performance, and one full-length NNAT® Level D practice test that students can use to assess their knowledge and practice their test-taking skills.

## Who Takes the NNAT® Level D?

The NNAT® Level D is often used as an assessment tool or admissions test in 3rd grade for entry into 4th grade of gifted and talented programs and highly-competitive schools. The NNAT® Level D is also used as an assessment tool by teachers to figure out which students would benefit from an accelerated or remedial curriculum.

## When Does the NNAT® Take Place?

This depends on the school district you reside in or want to attend. Check with the relevant school/ district to learn more about test dates and the application/ registration process.

## NNAT® Level D Overview

The NNAT® is designed to assess the cognitive skills that relate to academic success in school for students between four and 18. The questions on the NNAT® consist of geometric figures, shapes, and symbols. A child must use visual reasoning and logical thinking to decipher the answers. The test does not require a child to be able to read, write or speak in the English Language.

## Length

The NNAT® has 48 multiple-choice questions and offers both an online version and a paper and pencil test. It takes approximately 30 minutes to complete.

## Format

The official NNAT® test has only 3 colors: blue, orange and green. (The color green was recently added in the most recent edition of the NNAT).

# Part 2: How to Use this Book

The NNAT® is an important test and the more a student is familiar with the questions on the exam, the better she will fare when taking the test.

This book will help your student get used to the format and content of the test so s/he will be adequately prepared and feel confident on test day.

Inside this book, you will find:

- Overview of each question type on the test and teaching tips to help your child approach each question type strategically and with confidence.

- 1 full-length NNAT® Level D practice test and answer keys.

# Part 3. Test Prep Tips and Strategies

Firstly, and most importantly, commit to make the test preparation process a stress-free one. A student's ability to keep calm and focused in the face of challenge is a quality that will benefit him or her throughout his or her academic life.

Be prepared for difficult questions from the get-go! There will be a certain percentage of questions that are very challenging for all children. It is key to encourage students to use all strategies available when faced with challenging questions. And remember that a student can get quite a few questions wrong and still do very well on the test.

Before starting the practice test, go through the sample questions and read the general test prep strategies provided at the beginning of the book. They will help you guide your student as he or she progresses through the practice test.

The following general strategies may also be useful as you help your child prepare:

## Before You Start

- Find a quiet, comfortable spot to work free of distractions.
- Tell your student s/he will be doing some fun activities.
- Show your student how to perform the simple technique of shading (and erasing) bubbles.

## During Prep

- Encourage your student to carefully consider all the answer options before selecting one. Tell him or her there is only ONE answer.
- If your student is stumped by a question, she or he can use the process of elimination. First, encourage your student to eliminate obviously wrong answers to narrow down the answer choices. If your student is still in doubt after using this technique, tell him or her to guess as there are no points deducted for wrong answers.
- Encourage your student to visualise the correct answer in the empty box before checking the answer options.
- If challenged by a question, ask your student to explain why he or she chose a specific

answer. If the answer was incorrect, this will help you identify where your student is stumbling. If the answer was correct, asking your child to articulate her reasoning aloud will help reinforce the concept.

- Review all the questions your student answered incorrectly, and explain to your student why the answer is incorrect. Have your student attempt these questions again a few days later to see if he or she now understands the concept.
- Encourage your student to do his or her best, but take plenty of study breaks. Start with 10-15 minute sessions. Your student will perform best if she views these activities as fun and engaging, not as exercises to be avoided.

## When to Start Preparing?

Every family and student will approach preparation for this test differently. There is no 'right' way to prepare; there is only the best way for a particular child and family. We suggest students take one full-length practice test and spend 6-8 hours reviewing NNAT® practice questions.

If you have limited time to prepare, spend most energy reviewing areas where your student is encountering the majority of problems.

As they say, knowledge is power! Preparing for the NNAT® will certainly help your student avoid anxiety and make sure she does not give up too soon when faced with unfamiliar and perplexing questions.

# Part 4: Question Types and Teaching Tips

The NNAT® Level D is comprised of four different question types:

**Pattern Completion**
**Reasoning by Analogy**
**Serial Reasoning**
**Spatial Visualization**

Each question type involves the following steps:

- The student is presented with a picture of a matrix.
- The student must observe and detect the relationship among the parts of the matrix.
- The student must solve the problem based on the information shown to her within the matrix, and choose the correct answer from five possible options.

## Pattern Completion

With this question type, the student is presented with a design in a rectangle. Inside the large rectangle is a smaller white rectangle representing a missing piece that completes the design. The student must choose the answer that best fits the inner rectangle so that the missing parts complete the design.

These questions are the most common question types found on the Level A and B tests, and are the easiest kinds of matrices in the exam. On the Level D exam, there are relatively fewer of these question types.

**When your student first sees this kind of question, you can say to him/her:**

"Look at the picture. A piece is missing where you see the question mark. Show me the piece that is missing in the answer choices."

After seeing a few of these question types, your student will probably not need this prompt and will spontaneously point to or mark an answer.

SAMPLE QUESTION:

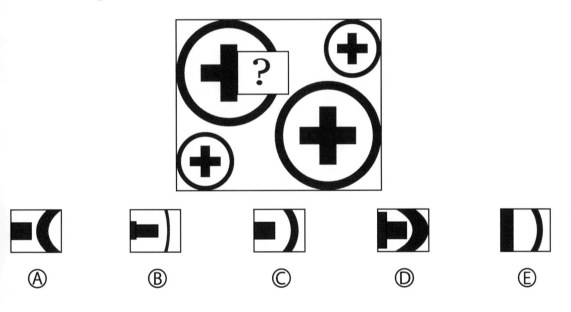

Ⓐ       Ⓑ       Ⓒ       Ⓓ       Ⓔ

**Answer: C**

## TIPS:

Ask your student to complete the picture by continuing the correct lines and colors of the design into the empty box. Then, match the drawing with the correct answer choice.

Ask your student to note the color/shade and design next to the corners of the empty box as this is a useful base to help identify the correct answer.

Go through each answer option and ask the student to visualize how each choice would fit the design.

# Reasoning by Analogy

With this question type, the child is presented with a matrix of 4-6 boxes containing objects, usually geometric shapes.

To solve the problem, the child must determine how the object changes as it moves across the row and down the column in the matrix. The question may require that the student pay close attention to several aspects of the design (e.g: shading, color, shape) at the same time.

**When your student first sees this kind of question, you can say to him/her:**

"Look at the picture. A piece is missing where you see the question mark. Show me the piece that is missing in the answer choices."

SAMPLE QUESTION:

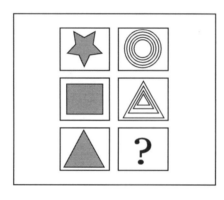

Ⓐ          Ⓑ          Ⓒ          Ⓓ          Ⓔ

**Answer: B**

## TIPS:

Make sure your student knows key concepts that come up in these types of questions, including geometric concepts such as rotational symmetry, line symmetry, parts of a whole.

If your student is finding these items difficult, encourage her to discover the pattern by looking in each direction (horizontally and vertically).
- Ask: "How do the objects change in the first row? Do you see a pattern? Do the objects change in the same way in the second row? The third row?"
- Ask: "How do the objects change in the first column? Do you see a pattern? Do the objects change in

the same way in the second column? The third column?"

**Encourage your student to isolate one element (e.g: outer shape, inner shape/s) and identify how it changes:**
- Is the color/shading of the element changing as it moves?
- Is the element changing positions as it moves? Does it move up or down? Clockwise or counter-clockwise? Does it end up in the opposite (mirror) position?
- Does the element disappear and appear again as it move along the row/ column? Does it get bigger or smaller?

**Encourage your student to make a prediction for the missing object and compare the description with the answer choices.**

## Serial Reasoning

With this question type, the student is shown a series of shapes that change across the rows and columns throughout the design. These questions require the student to understand how the objects in rows and columns relate to each other. The student must isolate and apply the rule/s in order to identify which object from the answer choices fits the empty box in the bottom right-hand corner of the matrix.

**When your student first sees this kind of question, you can say to him/her:**

"Look at the picture. A piece is missing where you see the question mark. Show me the piece that is missing in the answer choices."

SAMPLE QUESTION:

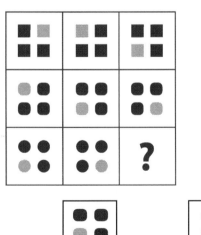

Ⓐ      Ⓑ      Ⓒ      Ⓓ      Ⓔ

**Answer: B**

## TIPS:

**Encourage your student to discover the pattern by looking in each direction.**

- Horizontally across the rows. Ask: "How do the objects change in the first row? Do you see a pattern? Do the objects change in the same way in the second row? The third row?"
- Vertically down the columns. Ask: "How do the objects change in the first column? Do you see a pattern? Do the objects change in the same way in the second column? The third column?"
- Diagonally (if the item is a 6-box matrix). Ask: "How do the objects change across the diagonal? Do you see a pattern?"

**Encourage your student to isolate one element (e.g: outer shape, inner shape/s) and identify how it changes.**

- How does the color/shading of the element change as it moves along the row/column?
- Does the element change positions as it moves along the row/column? Does it move up, down or around (i.e.: clockwise, counter-clockwise). Does the element move to the opposite position?
- Does the element get bigger, smaller or stay the same as it moves?
- Does the element disappear and appear again as you move along the row/column?

# Spatial Visualization

With this question type, a student is presented with a series of objects that com-bine, invert, transform and/or rotate across rows and columns. The student must identify the rule for the top row of objects and then predict what will happen to objects in the second (or third) row. S/he must then select which object among the answer choices follows this rule and should go in the empty box in the matrix.

Spatial Visualization items are widely seen to be the most difficult, particularly when involving objects that intersect in ways that are hard to recognize or involve an object rotating.

**When your student first sees this kind of question, you can say to him/her:**

"Look at the picture. A piece is missing where you see the question mark. Show me the piece that is missing in the answer choices."

SAMPLE QUESTION:

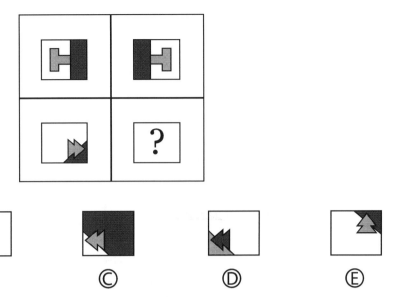

**Answer: A**

**TIPS:**
Ask your student to do some paper-folding projects. This will help her understand how objects on a folded piece of paper appear (and relate to each other) when the paper is opened.

Encourage your student to visualize -- observe, imagine and keep track of -- the changes in the geometric shapes as they move and then ask her to draw her prediction for what might be the correct shape/pattern to go in the empty box with the question mark.

Encourage your student to isolate one element (e.g: outer shape, inner shape/s) and identify how it changes

- How does the color/shading of the element change as it moves along the row/column?
- Does the element change positions as it moves along the row/column?Does the element move to the opposite position?
- Does the element flip positions (e.g.: outer square becomes inner square or vice-versa)? Does the element go upside down?
- Does the element combine with another element?

# NNAT® Level D
# Practice Test Two

NOTE: Answer bubble sheets can be found at the back of the book. Please make sure your student fills in each of the bubbles fully.

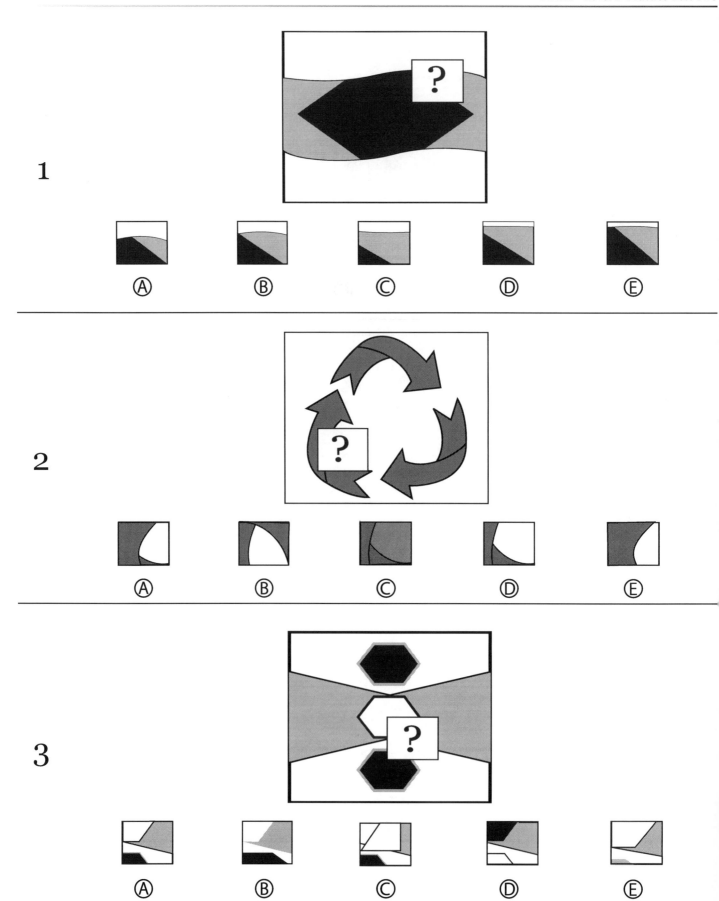

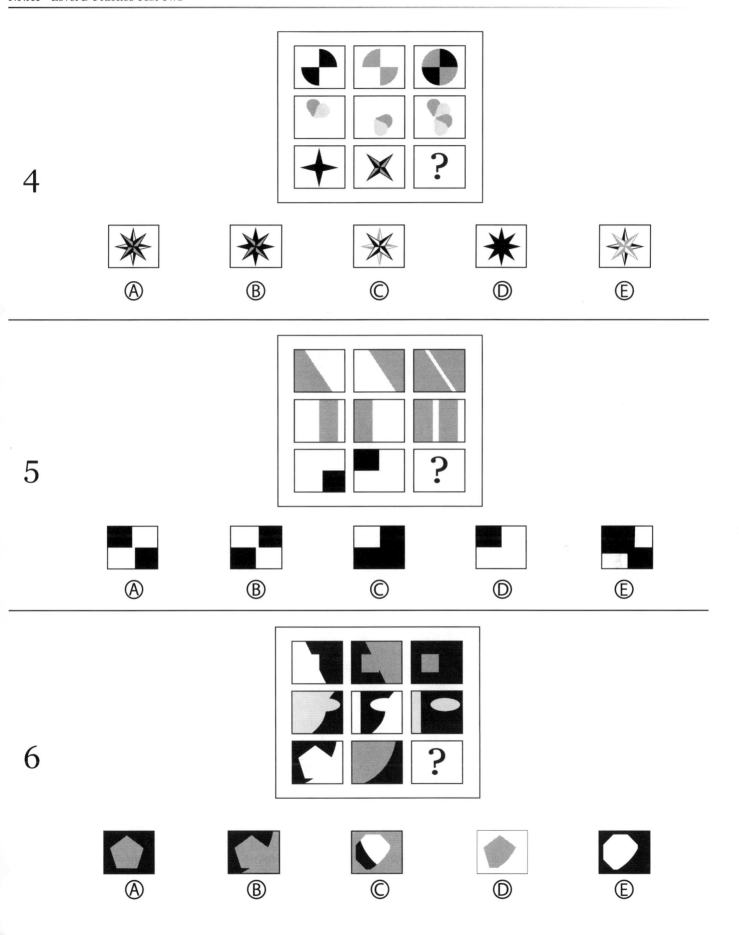

4

5

6

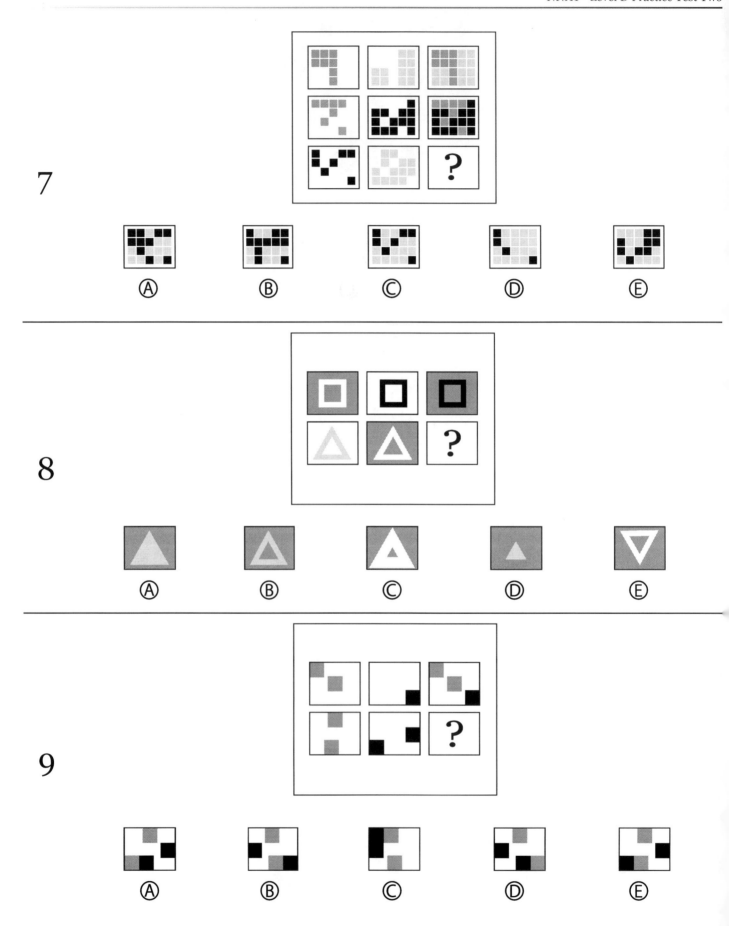

7

A    B    C    D    E

8

A    B    C    D    E

9

A    B    C    D    E

**10**

**11**

**12**

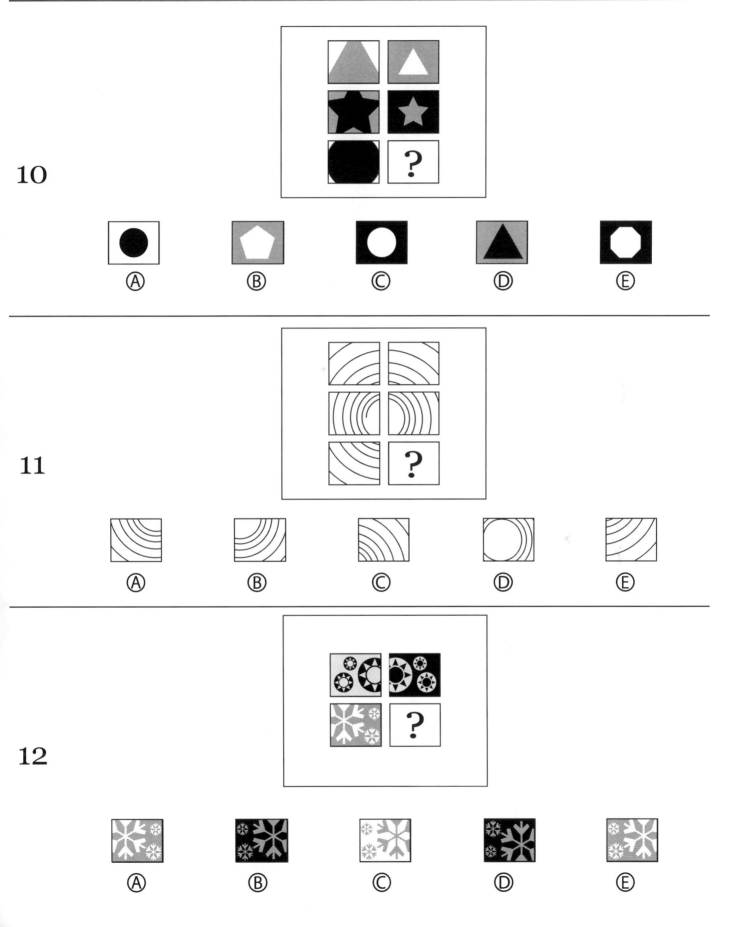

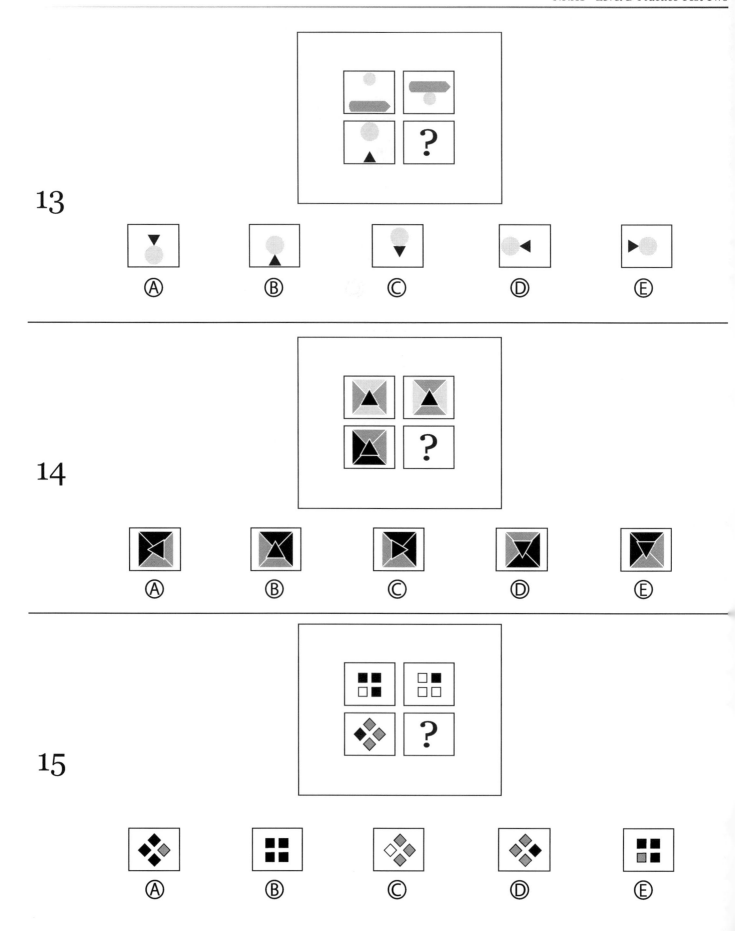

13

14

15

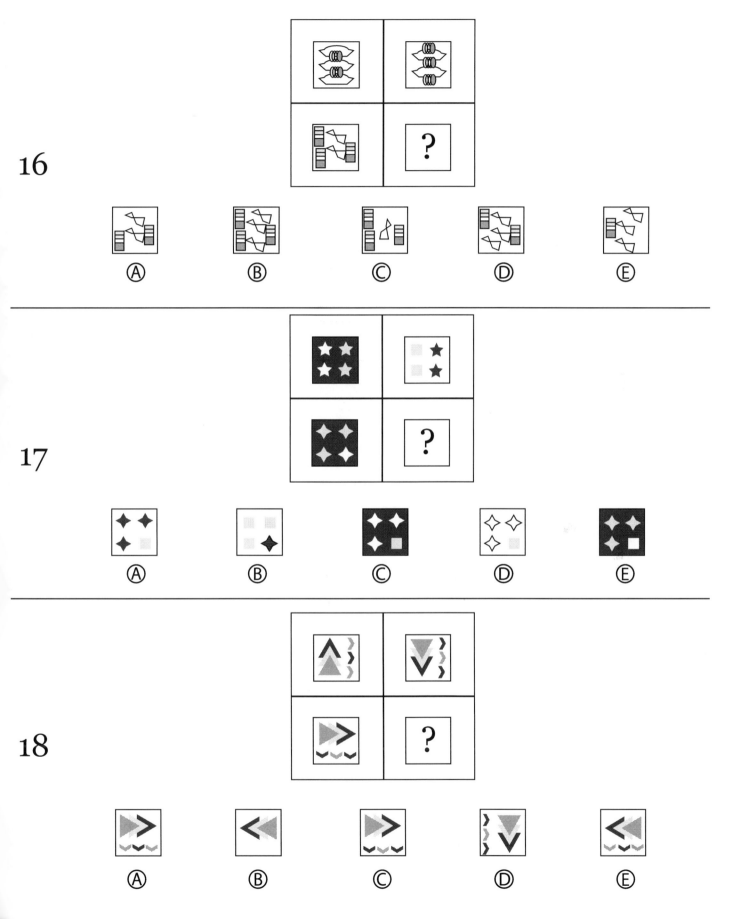

16

17

18

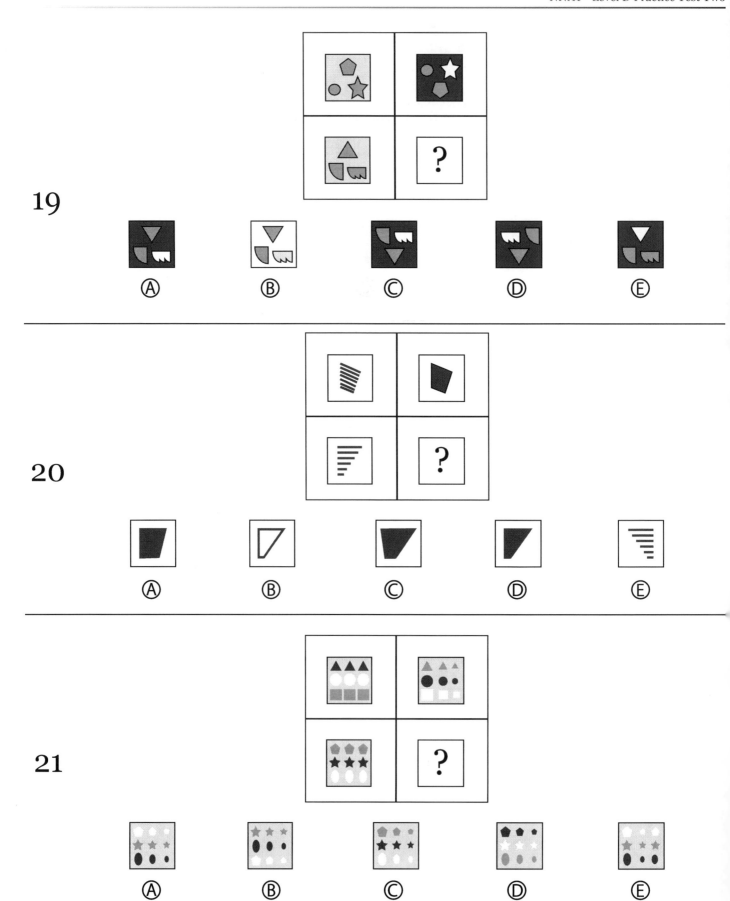

19

20

21

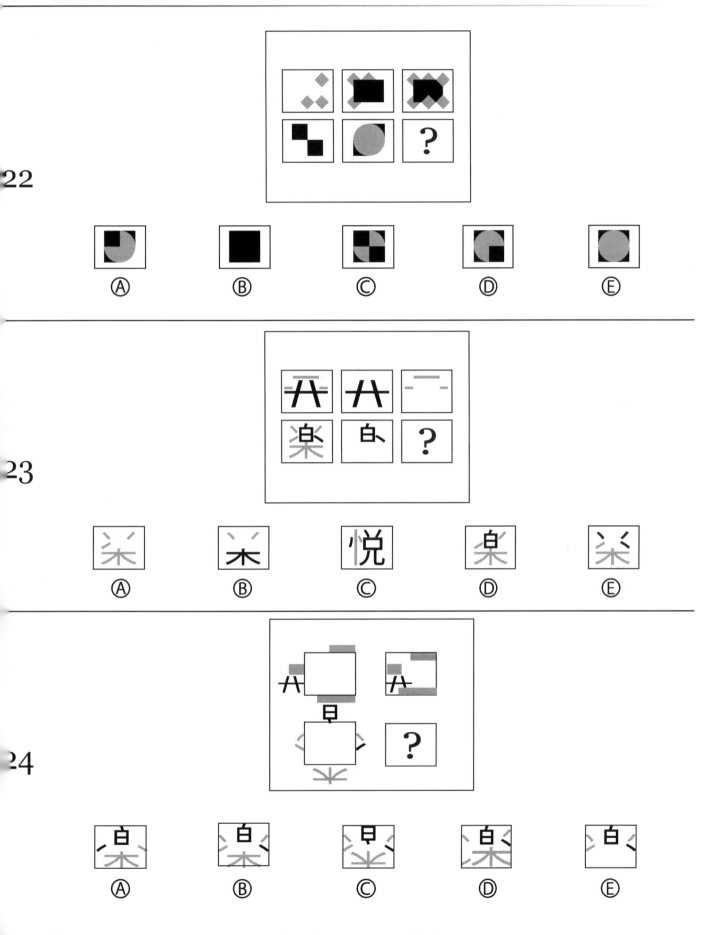

22

23

24

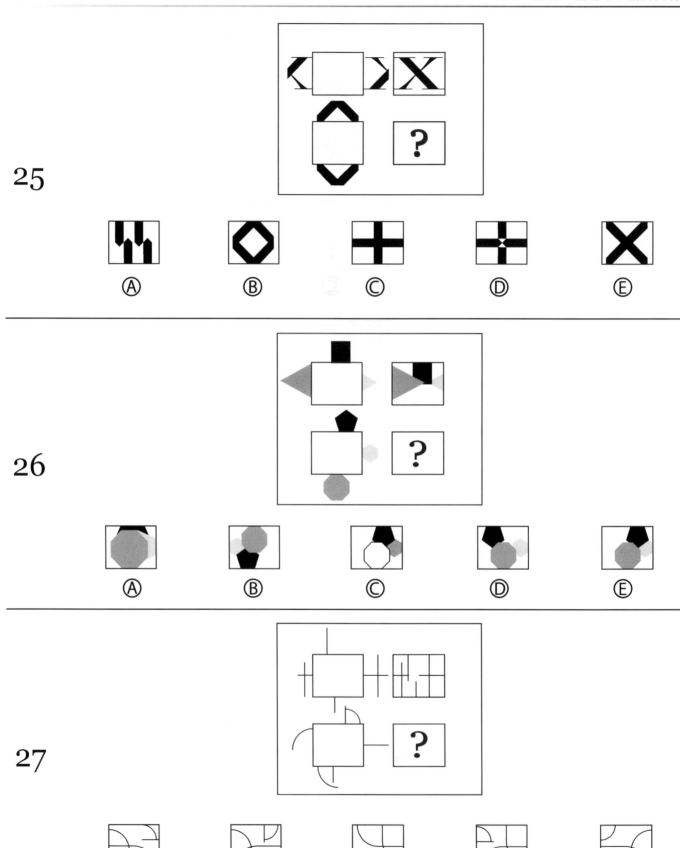

25

A B C D E

26

A B C D E

27

A B C D E

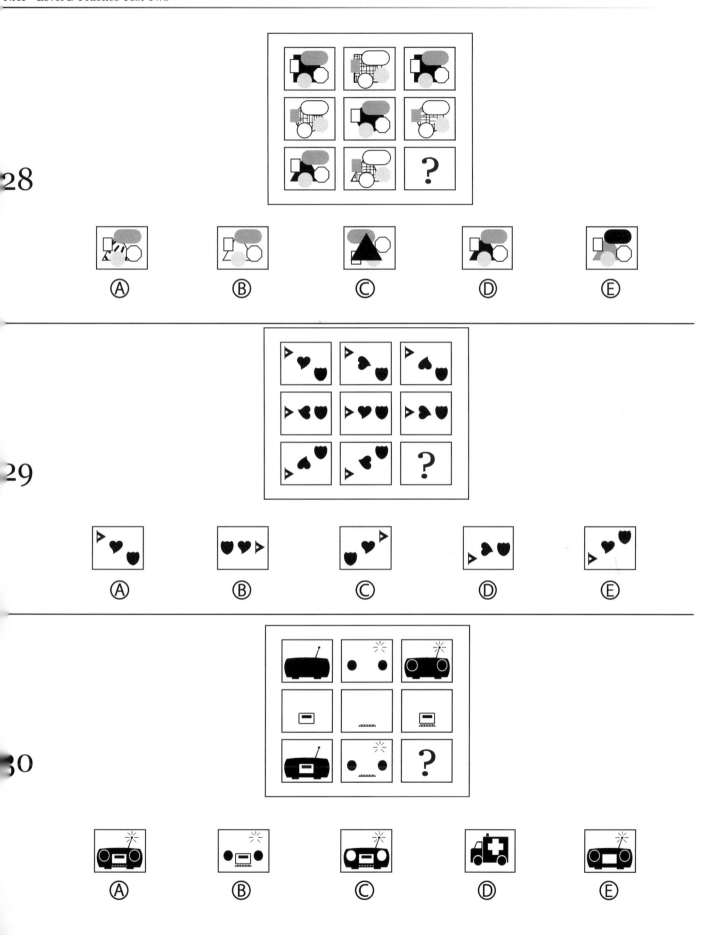

28

29

30

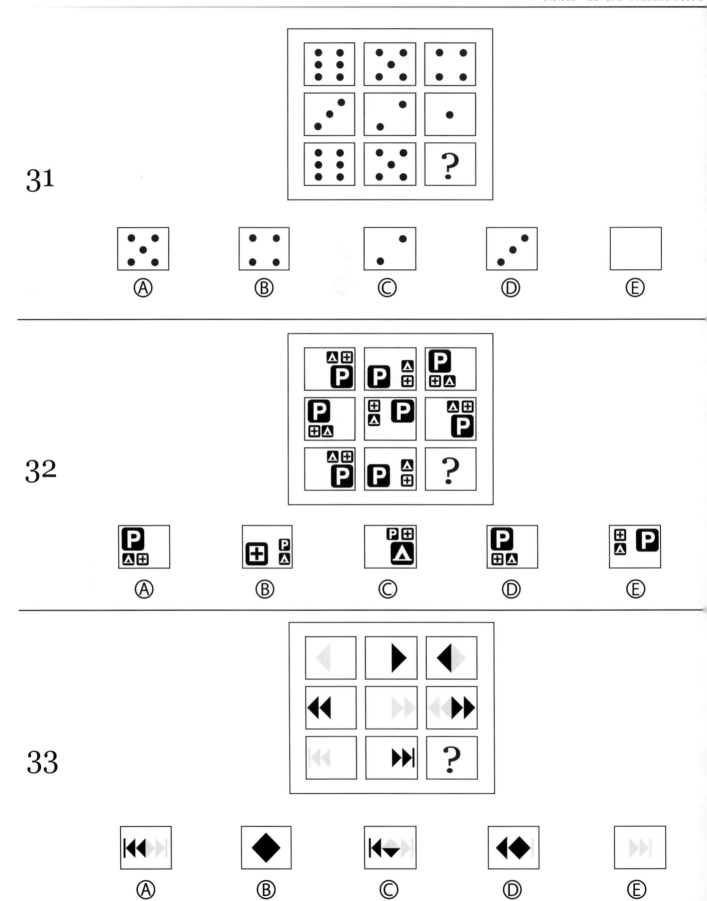

**31**

**32**

**33**

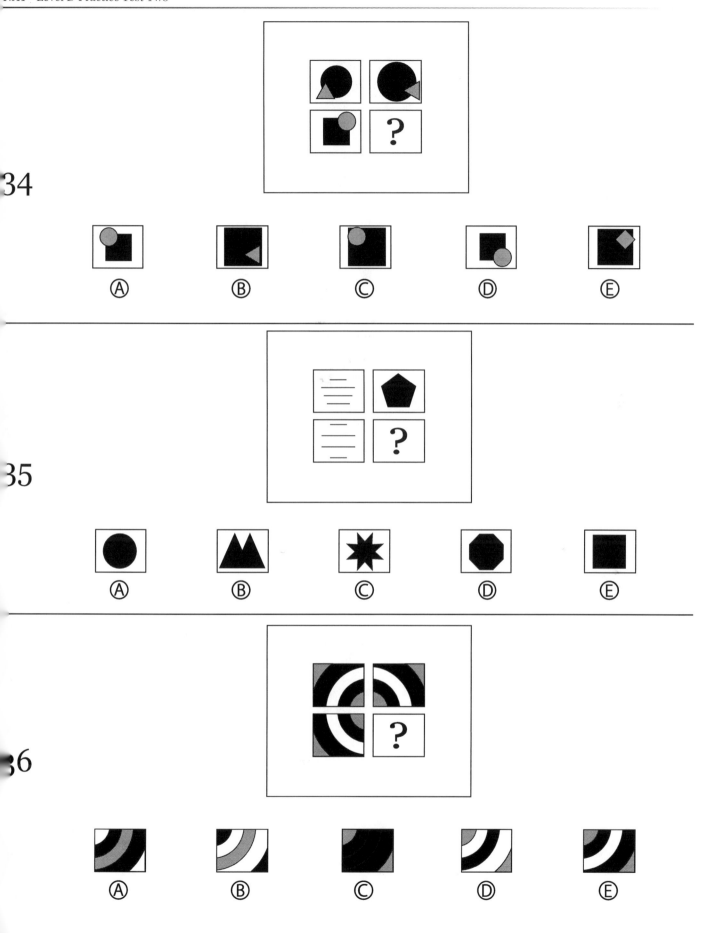

34

35

36

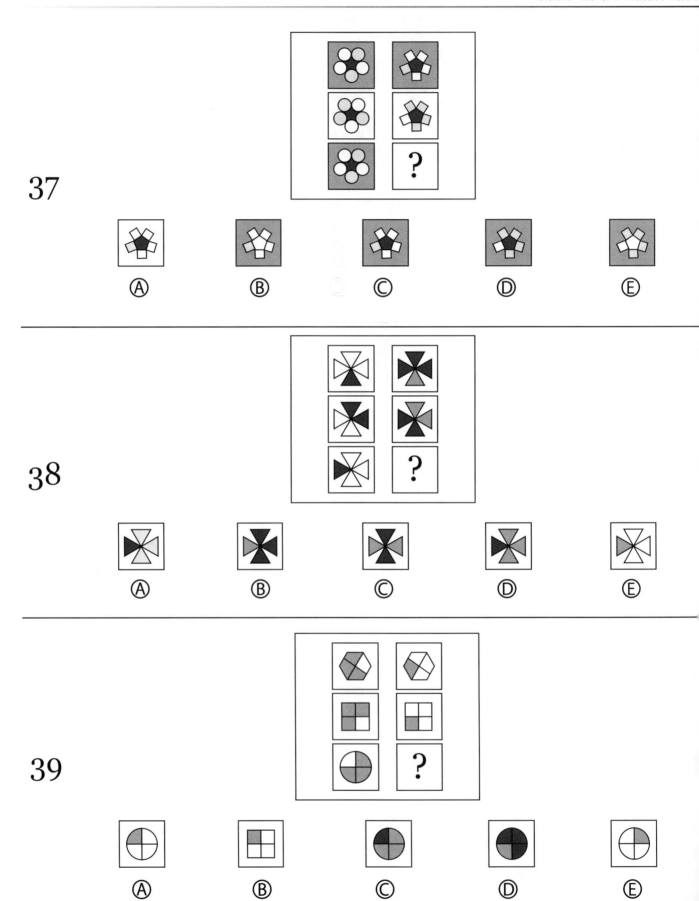

37

38

39

NNAT® Level D Test Prep Workbook Origins Publications

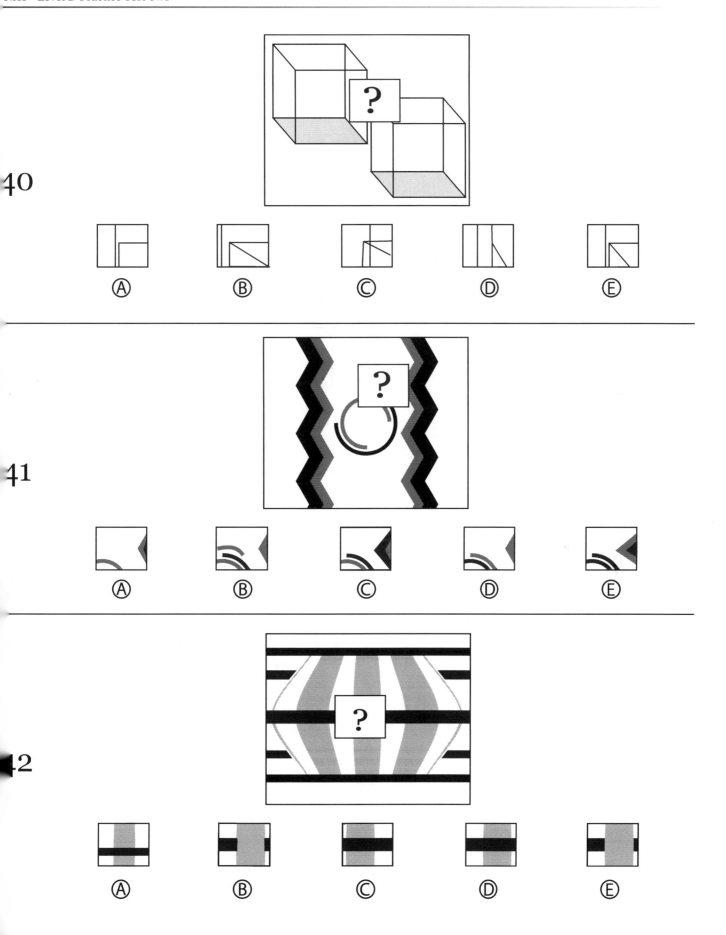

40

42

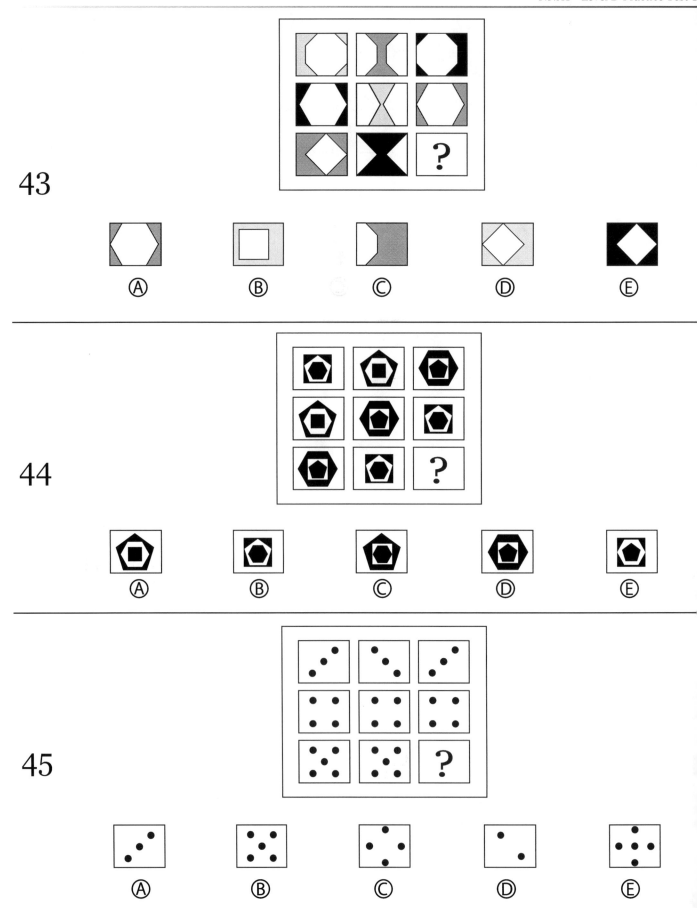

43

44

45

Origins Publications,

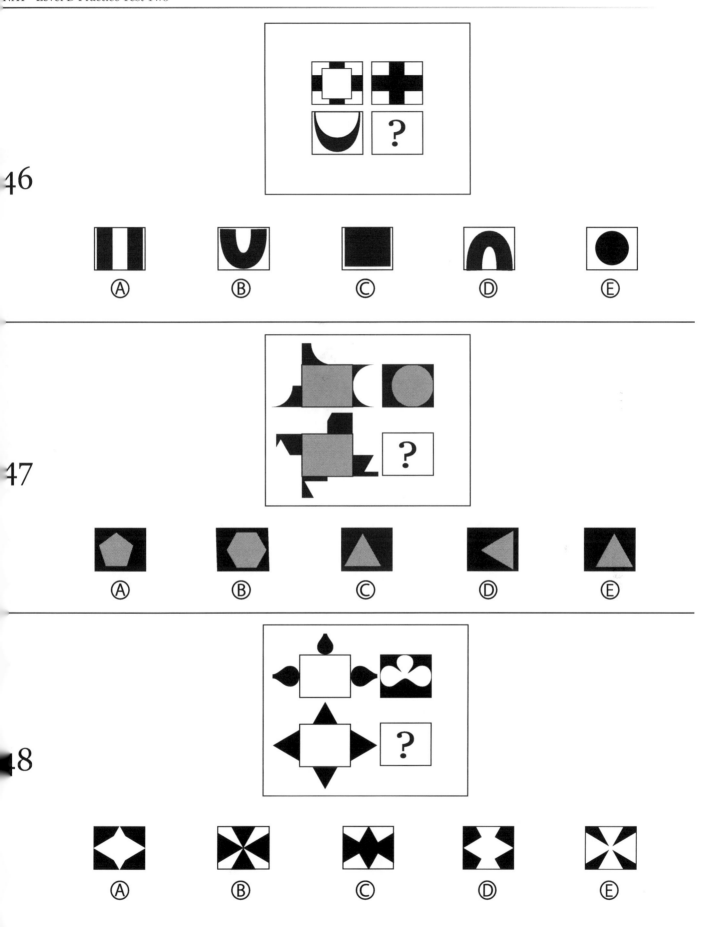

46

47

48

# NNAT® Level D
# Bubble Sheet
# & Answers

# Practice Test

Use a No. 2 Pencil
Fill in bubble completely.

Ⓐ ● Ⓒ Ⓓ

Name:_____     Date:_____

1. Ⓐ Ⓑ Ⓒ Ⓓ Ⓔ          26. Ⓐ Ⓑ Ⓒ Ⓓ Ⓔ
2. Ⓐ Ⓑ Ⓒ Ⓓ Ⓔ          27. Ⓐ Ⓑ Ⓒ Ⓓ Ⓔ
3. Ⓐ Ⓑ Ⓒ Ⓓ Ⓔ          28. Ⓐ Ⓑ Ⓒ Ⓓ Ⓔ
4. Ⓐ Ⓑ Ⓒ Ⓓ Ⓔ          29. Ⓐ Ⓑ Ⓒ Ⓓ Ⓔ
5. Ⓐ Ⓑ Ⓒ Ⓓ Ⓔ          30. Ⓐ Ⓑ Ⓒ Ⓓ Ⓔ
6. Ⓐ Ⓑ Ⓒ Ⓓ Ⓔ          31. Ⓐ Ⓑ Ⓒ Ⓓ Ⓔ
7. Ⓐ Ⓑ Ⓒ Ⓓ Ⓔ          32. Ⓐ Ⓑ Ⓒ Ⓓ Ⓔ
8. Ⓐ Ⓑ Ⓒ Ⓓ Ⓔ          33. Ⓐ Ⓑ Ⓒ Ⓓ Ⓔ
9. Ⓐ Ⓑ Ⓒ Ⓓ Ⓔ          34. Ⓐ Ⓑ Ⓒ Ⓓ Ⓔ
10. Ⓐ Ⓑ Ⓒ Ⓓ Ⓔ         35. Ⓐ Ⓑ Ⓒ Ⓓ Ⓔ
11. Ⓐ Ⓑ Ⓒ Ⓓ Ⓔ         36. Ⓐ Ⓑ Ⓒ Ⓓ Ⓔ
12. Ⓐ Ⓑ Ⓒ Ⓓ Ⓔ         37. Ⓐ Ⓑ Ⓒ Ⓓ Ⓔ
13. Ⓐ Ⓑ Ⓒ Ⓓ Ⓔ         38. Ⓐ Ⓑ Ⓒ Ⓓ Ⓔ
14. Ⓐ Ⓑ Ⓒ Ⓓ Ⓔ         39. Ⓐ Ⓑ Ⓒ Ⓓ Ⓔ
15. Ⓐ Ⓑ Ⓒ Ⓓ Ⓔ         40. Ⓐ Ⓑ Ⓒ Ⓓ Ⓔ
16. Ⓐ Ⓑ Ⓒ Ⓓ Ⓔ         41. Ⓐ Ⓑ Ⓒ Ⓓ Ⓔ
17. Ⓐ Ⓑ Ⓒ Ⓓ Ⓔ         42. Ⓐ Ⓑ Ⓒ Ⓓ Ⓔ
18. Ⓐ Ⓑ Ⓒ Ⓓ Ⓔ         43. Ⓐ Ⓑ Ⓒ Ⓓ Ⓔ
19. Ⓐ Ⓑ Ⓒ Ⓓ Ⓔ         44. Ⓐ Ⓑ Ⓒ Ⓓ Ⓔ
20. Ⓐ Ⓑ Ⓒ Ⓓ Ⓔ         45. Ⓐ Ⓑ Ⓒ Ⓓ Ⓔ
21. Ⓐ Ⓑ Ⓒ Ⓓ Ⓔ         46. Ⓐ Ⓑ Ⓒ Ⓓ Ⓔ
22. Ⓐ Ⓑ Ⓒ Ⓓ Ⓔ         47. Ⓐ Ⓑ Ⓒ Ⓓ Ⓔ
23. Ⓐ Ⓑ Ⓒ Ⓓ Ⓔ         48. Ⓐ Ⓑ Ⓒ Ⓓ Ⓔ
24. Ⓐ Ⓑ Ⓒ Ⓓ Ⓔ
25. Ⓐ Ⓑ Ⓒ Ⓓ Ⓔ

# NNAT D Answer Explanations.

*Please note that there are often various ways to solve the puzzles. These answer explantions provide one option for solving each puzzle.*

*The answer explanations provide the correct answer for both the 'color' and 'black and white' versions of the book (the black/white/ gray shade are referenced, when relevant, in brackets).*

*Download a color version of this book at:* **https://originstutoring.lpages.co/nnat150**

1. **B.** The puzzle piece completes the pattern.

2. **D.** The puzzle piece completes the pattern.

3. **A.** The puzzle piece completes the pattern.

4. **B.** The second column stacks on top of the first to form the final figure in the third column.

5. **A.** The first and second shapes in each row combine to form the final third shape.

6. **A.** The shapes combine from left to right and assume the non white background color. Down the third column, the background of the boxes are black.

7. **C.** The shaded grids combine from left to right to complete the grids in the third column.

8. **B.** The shaded figures combine from left to right to complete the figures on the right, with white transparent when combined.

9. **E.** In each row, the squares from column 1 combine with the squares from column 2 to become column 3.

10. **C.** The shape is reduced while the colors are inverted.

11. **E.** The lines complete the spiral mural.

12. **C.** In the second column, the figures are reflected vertically and the colors are inverted.

13. **A.** The figures meet at the horizon and then reflect on the horizon.

14. **B.** The background shapes invert colors, while the topmost shape remains the same.

15. **A.** The figures are rotated 180 degrees, and the colors are inverted.

16. **D.** Moving from the left to right box in the top row, the shape with three figures decreases by one and the shape with two figures (colored rings) increases by one. The bottom boxes must reflect the same relationship.

17. **A.** Moving from left to right box, the background color changes to white, the white stars change to light blue (light gray) squares, and the light blue (light gray) stars change to dark blue (black) stars. The bottom boxes must reflect the same relationship. Therefore A is correct.

18. **E.** Moving from the left to right box, the position of the arrowheads are left undisturbed, but the arrowheads swap their colors. The set of three triangles rotates 180 degrees but the triangles' colo are retained.

19. **C.** Moving from the left to right box, the background color changes to dark blue (black), the shape at the top moves to the bottom and it is rotated 180 degrees. The shape at the bottom right changes its color to white and moves to the top, th shape at the bottom left retains its color and move to the top.

20. **D.** Moving from the left to right box, the lines form a shape filled with dark blue (black) color.

21. **A.** Moving from the left to right box, the dark blue (black) changes to orange (medium gray), white changes to black, and orange (medium gray) changes to white. The size of the left column of shapes remains the same, while the shapes in the middle column becomes medium sized, and the shapes in the right column becomes small sized.

22. **C.** The figures in the first column stack on the figures in the second column to complete the figur in the third column.

23. **A.** The figure in the first column is divided int its components by color from left to right.

4. **B.** The shapes fold inward on the left to create the final figure on the right.

5. **E.** The shapes on the left fold inward to create the figure on the right.

6. **E.** The shapes on the left fold in smallest to largest to create the final collage on the right, with the smallest shape on the bottom and the largest shape on top.

7. **B.** The lines fold from the outside on the left to the inside on the right to complete the collage.

8. **D.** The large background shapes alternate between black and a hatch pattern, while the smaller shapes alternate colors in pairs both vertically and horizontally.

9. **E.** The center shape rotates across each row and down each column, while the outer shapes move to opposite corners down the columns.

0. **A.** The shapes combine from left to right and from top to bottom to form the final object.

. **B.** The circles decrease in number from from left right by one. Down each column, the numbers dots alternates between two numbers: 626 in column one, 525 in column two, and 414 in column ree.

. **D.** All three objects move clockwise inside the ge of the enclosing square across the rows.

. **A.** The shapes combine across the rows while the t and right sides alternate in shade/color.

. **C.** The shapes rotate 80 degrees unterclockwise while the background image creases in size.

. **D.** The lines in the left column, if surrounded by outside line, form the shape in the right column.

. **E.** The bottom right figure completes the larger ural.

. **C.** Down the column, the pattern alternates tween two patterns: the color of the inner star mains the same, while the surrounding circles ap their colors. The background frame alternates or between two colors.

38. **B.** Moving from the left to right box, dark blue (black) triangle changes to orange (gray) and the white triangles change to dark blue (black).

39. **E.** Moving from the top left to right box, the shape is flipped horizontally and the colors are swapped.

40. **E.** The puzzle piece completes the pattern.

41. **B.** The puzzle piece completes the pattern.

42. **D.** The puzzle piece completes the pattern.

43. **D.** The foreground shape is mirrored across the rows while the background alternates across and down between black, mint green (light gray) and orange (medium gray).

44. **A.** The stacking order of the three shapes alternates across and down, but the top and bottom shapes are always black.

45. **B.** Each row rotates 90 degrees.

46. **B.** The foreground shape is removed from the left column to reveal the background shape in the right column.

47. **C.** The shapes on the left fold inward, forming a figure to one side with the background color showing through.

48. **E.** The shapes on the left fold inward and the colors of the resulting collage on the right are inverted.

# DOWNLOAD THE PRACTICE TESTS
## IN COLOR

If you also want the COLOR version of this book, please go to the following link to download it!

Please visit
**https://originstutoring.lpages.co/nnat150**
to access a color version of your practice tests.

**Thank you for selecting this book.
We would be thrilled if you left us a review on the website where you bought this book!**

Made in United States
Troutdale, OR
09/22/2024

23042506R00022